"If you're gonna make a dream come true, you gotta work it.

You can't just sit around."

On a cold, snowy day
in a one-room cabin
tucked between two tall Tennessee mountains,
Dolly Parton was born.
And before you could holler, "Howdy neighbor!"
she began squallin' so loud
her powerful voice shook them mountains. (Well, almost!)

Now Dolly's parents didn't have two nickels
to pay the doctor
who brought their squallin' baby into the world.
So they gave him a sack of cornmeal instead.
Her family was more than dirt poor.
They were newspaper-pasted-over-drafty-walls poor.

In time, Dolly's mighty squallin'
turned into marvelous singin'.
At her granddaddy's church, she sang soulful hymns
with tambourines shakin' and people shoutin'.
Soon, she dreamed of becoming a singin' star!

Music filled Dolly's heart so plumb full
she had to let it out.
When geese soared overhead,
she snapped her fingers to their honkin' beat,
and performed a goose-honkin' song.

When a bobwhite called out at night,
she used his notes
to create a sweet lullaby.

And when Mama snapped beans,
Dolly pounded a pot with a spoon
and belted out her bean-snappin' tune.
But Daddy didn't take kindly
to his daughter dawdling with tunes
instead of pulling prickly weeds.

Dolly never had fancy, store-bought toys.
But she didn't mind.
'Cause she had a heap of
brothers and sisters to play with—
Willadeene, David, Denver,
Bobby, Stella, Cassie,
plus more babies through the years—
a dozen Parton kids in all.

Mama made her a corncob doll
with shiny corn-silk hair
and a corn-shuck dress.
Dolly named her Tiny Tasseltop
and sang to her at the top of her lungs.

Now Dolly understood a songwritin' star
should have her own guitar.
Fortunately, she knew how to take next-to-nothin'
and create a special-somethin'.
Dolly found some rusty piano strings
and strung up an old, discarded mandolin.
After that, she spent every spare second
strumming and composing songs.

Dolly's dazzlin' talent shone
like a thousand fireflies on a moonless night.
After learning to play guitar chords,
she used those chords to create guitar licks.
Then, arranged them licks into toe-tappin',
sad-sappin' songs.

"I started writing songs before I could even write."

Perched on her front-porch stage
with a tin can microphone,
Dolly performed for anyone she could corral—
a bunch of baby siblings ('til they crawled away),
a flock of ducks ('til they waddled away),
and a pen of pigs (fortunately, they couldn't get away!).

Yet, she dreamed of performing for a real audience.

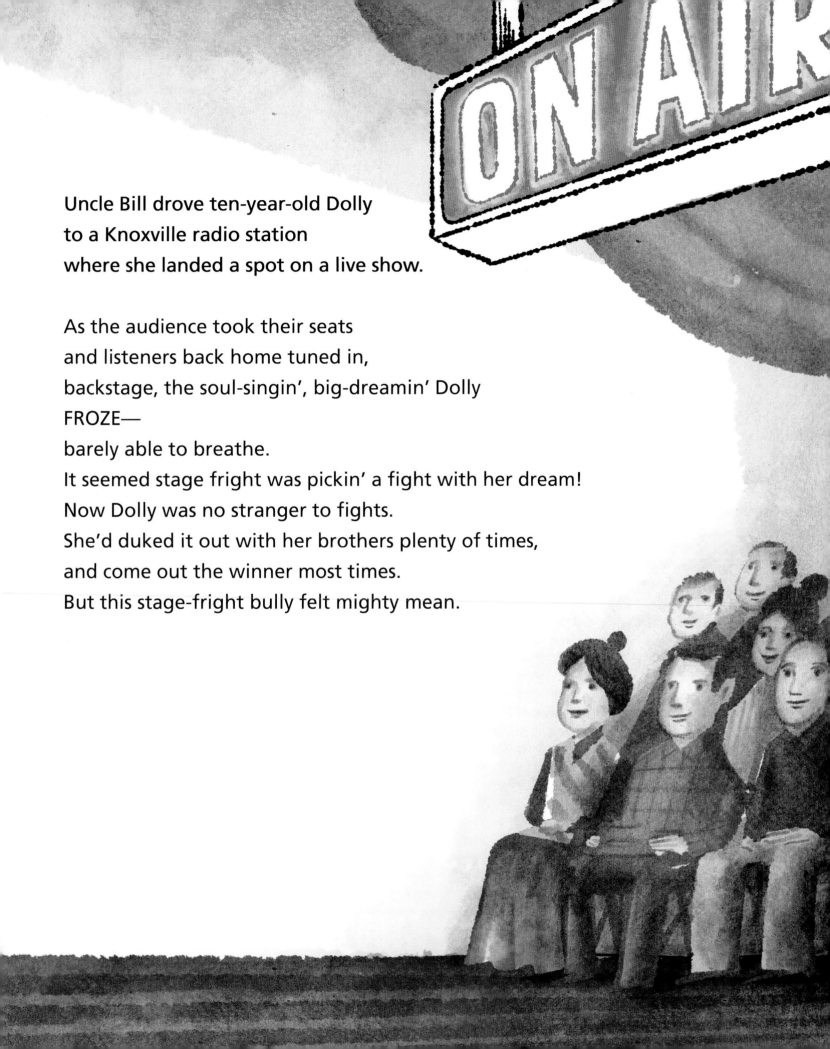

Uncle Bill drove ten-year-old Dolly
to a Knoxville radio station
where she landed a spot on a live show.

As the audience took their seats
and listeners back home tuned in,
backstage, the soul-singin', big-dreamin' Dolly
FROZE—
barely able to breathe.
It seemed stage fright was pickin' a fight with her dream!
Now Dolly was no stranger to fights.
She'd duked it out with her brothers plenty of times,
and come out the winner most times.
But this stage-fright bully felt mighty mean.

Dolly knew if she didn't stand up to it
her dream might die.
So she marched over to the microphone,
opened her quivering mouth,
and sang a few notes—real quiet-like,
then a little louder,
'til she squashed that stage fright
like a pesky June bug.

When she finished,
the crowd demanded an encore.
But she'd only rehearsed one song.
So, she sang it again!

"I had this something
that kept pushing me forward,
even when I was so scared....
It was something I
had to do."

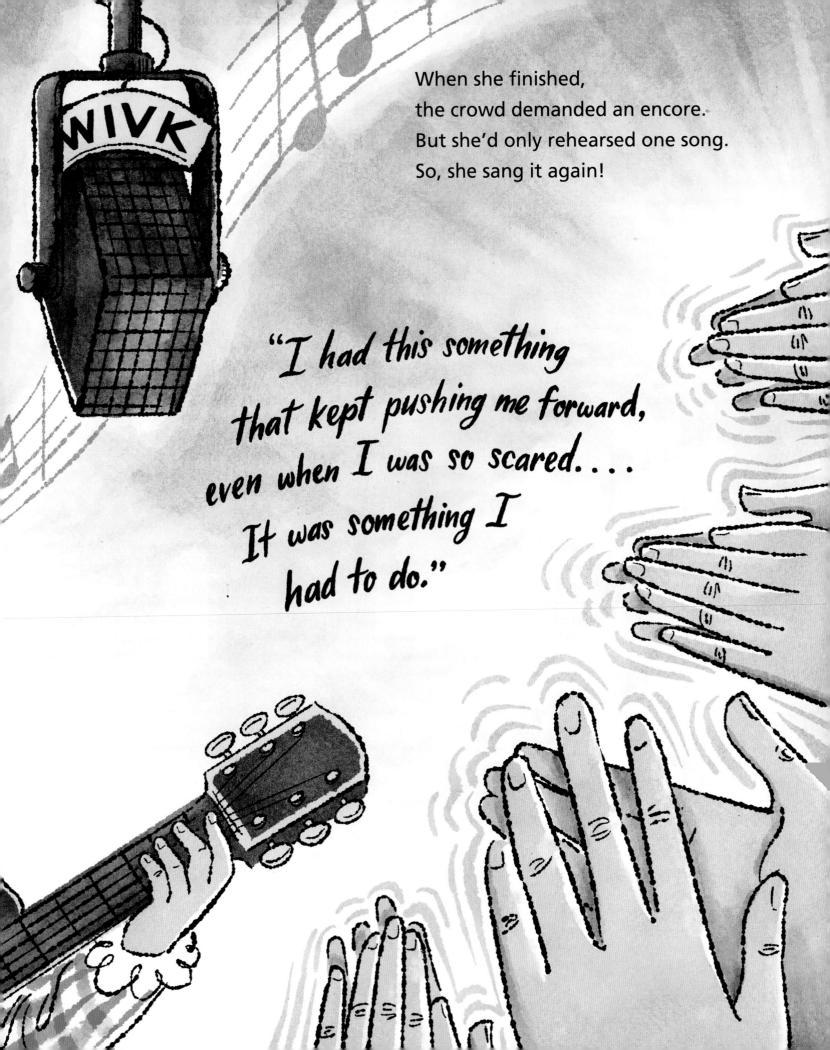

The audience loved Dolly's incredible voice.
So the producer invited her to perform
on his live television program.
Soon, she had a regular gig on the show.
While it lasted,
small-town Dolly earned big-city money—
five dollars a show!

Dolly fixed her sights on the BIG stage—
the Grand Ole Opry in Nashville,
where top country singers performed.
With her uncle by her side,
she traipsed up and down town—
pleadin' with singers to give up their slot
and give her a shot
on that Opry stage.
She got lots of no's
then finally wrangled a yes.

Legendary singer Johnny Cash
introduced thirteen-year-old Dolly at the Opry:
"We've got a little girl here
from up in East Tennessee."

Weak-kneed,
Dolly stepped in front of
the brightest lights and biggest audience
she'd ever seen.
And wouldn't you know—at that *very* moment
the stage-fright bully showed up again.

"I was scared to death....
My desire to do it was always greater
than my fear."

But Dolly had tussled with this bully before
and knew right what to do.
She simply smiled,
and began singin' for her mama and daddy
listening on their radio back in the holler.

She sang for God
and she sang for her dream,
which she *knew* would come true.
The crowd cheered for an encore.
Then another. And another!

Sure as pokeberry blooms in summer,
Dolly began blossoming and sprouting too
(all the way to five foot two!).
She bleached her hair
and put on makeup
just like them models in magazines.

Dolly's parents didn't like their
starry-eyed daughter
with blond hair piled high to the sky
runnin' off to nearby towns
strummin' and singin'.

So Dolly agreed
to stay home during the week
doing schoolwork and chores.
But on the weekends
her parents couldn't stop her
from performin'.

Dolly and her uncle got real good
at parking themselves in music studios,
like possums in a garbage can,
until Dolly was allowed to audition.
They once spent an entire day
fast-talking a record producer into listening to Dolly.
When he finally agreed,
her powerful voice knocked his socks clean off,
and he offered her a one-record deal!

When Dolly heard her very own voice
on the hometown station,
she was tickled three shades of pink.
Other local radio stations played her record too.

Then overnight, them stations turned fickle.
They started playing top hits instead of her song.
Listeners forgot all about Dolly—and her music.
But she was determined to keep chasin' her dream!

At Dolly's high school graduation,
Mama beamed with pride,
squirmy young'uns on both sides,
while Daddy stayed home to plow fields.
Each student shared their plans.
Some were headin' off to college.
Others were gettin' hitched.
When it came Dolly's turn, she announced,
"I'm going to Nashville to be a star."
Laughter filled the room.
Dolly was puzzled—and angry!
Hadn't they heard her sing?

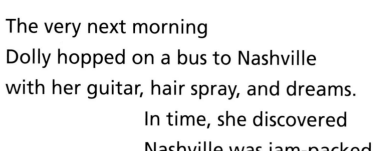

The very next morning
Dolly hopped on a bus to Nashville
with her guitar, hair spray, and dreams.
In time, she discovered
Nashville was jam-packed with hopeful singers
trying to make a living, just like her.
But music was her passion—her *life*.
So hungry, homesick, and flat broke,
Dolly kept on writin',
strummin',
and singin'.
Nothing was going to stop her
from runnin' full steam after her dream
(in high heels!).

And you know what?

Dolly finally caught that dream by the tail—
                        and she never let go!

"Year in and year out, a lot of my dreams that I planned— they come true."

More about Dolly

*"I hope to never retire. . . .
I wake up every day with new
dreams."*

Dolly Parton is an extraordinary performer and songwriter who has entertained audiences for six decades (and counting!). People also admire her warmth and honesty. Dolly got her first taste of performing when she sang in her grandpa's church. Later, she and her sisters sang in other local churches.

After high school, Dolly moved to Nashville to start her music career. Her first day in town, she met a boy named Carl Dean while waiting outside a Laundromat for her clothes to dry. They married two years later and have been together ever since. The two rarely appear in public together because Carl doesn't like the spotlight. The couple has no children, yet their lives are full with many nieces, nephews, extended family members, and friends.

A prolific songwriter, Dolly has composed more than three thousand songs. Each one tells a story—about life, feelings, dreams, and memories. Twenty-five of her songs became number one hits. She's sold more than one hundred million records around the world. Her best seller is "I Will Always Love You."

Dolly has found success in many music genres: country, pop, bluegrass, and gospel. She's won over a dozen Academy of Country Music Awards, eleven Grammy Awards, three American Music Awards, and an Emmy. She was the Country Music Association's Entertainer of the Year in 1978, and inducted into the Country Music Hall of Fame in 1999. Her acting career includes movie megahits *9 to 5* and *Steel Magnolias*, along with many television movies and shows. It's no wonder she has two stars on Hollywood's Walk of Fame!

Many singers have enjoyed collaborating with Dolly. Early in her career (the late 1960s to early '70s), she was a regular performer with Porter Wagoner on his TV show. Dolly worked with Linda Ronstadt and Emmylou Harris to create several hit albums together. She's also recorded songs with Kenny Rogers, Julio Iglesias, Willie Nelson, Billy Ray Cyrus, Queen Latifah, Vince Gill, Norah Jones, Brad Paisley, and many others.

A savvy businessperson, Dolly is the co-owner of dinner theaters, a water park, and her famous Dollywood Park. The park is located in Pigeon Forge, Tennessee, near where she grew up, and provides thousands of jobs for struggling families. She started Sandollar Productions in 1986, and has negotiated business deals with Time-Life, Netflix, Williams-Sonoma (think guitar-shaped cookies!), and more. She's written autobiographies and children's books, as well as her own cookbook.

Dolly's hard work, talent, and popularity have led to great wealth—which she takes great joy in sharing. "I've been blessed in my life to become a celebrity. And when you're in a position to help, you should help," she explained. Over the years, she's given millions to others.

Where Dolly grew up, Sevier County, Tennessee, poverty has been an ongoing problem. For years she provided band scholarships for Sevier County High School students. In 1988 she created the Dollywood Foundation, which offers college scholarships to seniors at local high schools. In 1991 she started the Buddy Program to reduce Sevier County's high school dropout rate (which was over 30 percent). To kick off the program, Dolly met with middle school students and explained how an education would help them achieve their dreams. She also offered each $500 if they earned a high school diploma. Her generous plan lowered the dropout rate to 6 percent!

As a child who loved to read, but didn't have the luxury of books in her home, Dolly believes it is important to provide children with their very own books. In 1995 she founded Imagination Library. So far, it's given more than one hundred fifty million books to children. Dolly created this literacy program to honor her daddy, who, she said, "couldn't read or write, but he was the smartest person that I've ever known."

Dolly has an empathetic heart and loves to help others. When devastating wildfires tore through Tennessee in 2016, she gave more than $3 million to families who'd lost their homes. When COVID-19 was spreading across the world in 2020, she donated $1 million to Vanderbilt University Medical Center, which worked with Moderna to help develop a vaccine. Just like Dolly pursued her dream, her kindness and generosity are helping people pursue and achieve theirs!

Timeline

January 19, 1946: Dolly Rebecca Parton is born in Sevierville, Tennessee.

1952: Writes her first song, "Little Tiny Tasseltop."

1956: Performs on the radio for *The Cas Walker Show* in Knoxville.

1959: Makes her first appearance at the Grand Ole Opry and sings "You Gotta Be My Baby."

1962: Records her first record for Mercury Records, "It May Not Kill Me (But It's Sure Gonna Hurt)."

May 1964: Graduates from Sevier County High School.

May 30, 1966: Marries Carl Dean.

1967: Begins appearing on *The Porter Wagoner Show*.

1967: Releases debut album, *Hello, I'm Dolly*.

1974: Releases three solo songs, "I Will Always Love You," "Jolene," and "Love Is Like a Butterfly." All become No. 1 hits on the country chart.

1977: Releases *Here You Come Again*, which becomes her first gold album.

1980: Stars in movie *9 to 5,* featuring the song she wrote of the same name.

1986: Opens Dollywood Park in Pigeon Forge, Tennessee.

1987: Releases *Trio*, her first collaborative album with Emmylou Harris and Linda Ronstadt. It reaches No. 1 on the country chart, wins a Grammy, and receives numerous other accolades.

1992: Whitney Houston records Dolly's song "I Will Always Love You" for *The Bodyguard* movie.

1995: Founds Imagination Library literacy program.

1999: Is inducted into the Country Music Hall of Fame.

2004: Accepts the Living Legend Medal from the Library of Congress.

2009: *9 to 5: The Musical*, with music and lyrics by Dolly, opens on Broadway.

2020: Documentary about Dolly's Imagination Library, *The Library That Dolly Built*, releases.

2021: Appears in the TIME100 World's Most Influential People of 2021.

2021: Receives three Guinness World Records: Most Hits on Billboard's Hot Country Songs Chart by a Female Artist; Most No. 1 Hits on Billboard's Hot Country Songs Chart by a Female Artist; and the Most Decades with a Top 20 Hit on Billboard's Hot Country Songs Chart.

2022: Nominated to be inducted into the Rock & Roll Hall of Fame.

Selected Bibliography

All quotations used in the book can be found in the following sources marked with an asterisk (*).

BOOKS

Parton, Dolly. *Dolly: My Life and Other Unfinished Business*. New York: HarperCollins Publishers, 1994.

VIDEOS

*Chapelle, Al, dir. *Dolly Parton: Queen of Country*. London: Entertain Me Productions Ltd, 2015.

*Library of Congress. "Dolly Parton Dedicates Her Imagination Library's 100 Millionth Book to the Library of Congress." 2018. loc.gov/item/webcast-8289.

*Live Nation TV and Hard Rock International. "Dolly Parton's Opry Debut" in *Encore: A Never-Ending Story*. August 24, 2016.

WEBSITES

*Dolly Parton, dollyparton.com.

Dolly Parton's Imagination Library, imaginationlibrary.com.

Dollywood, dollywood.com.

AUDIO

McEvers, Kelly, and Mary Louise Kelly. "Dolly Parton Recognized for 2 World Records in Country Music." *All Things Considered*. Washington, DC: National Public Radio, January 19, 2018. npr.org/2018/01/19/579227938.

NEWSPAPERS/MAGAZINES

*Butterworth, Lisa. "All Dolled Up." *BUST Magazine*, June/July 2014.

*Carroll, Nicole. "Dolly Parton: 'The whole magic about me is that I look artificial, but I'm totally real.'" *USA Today*, August 27, 2020.

Cramer, Maria. "Dolly Parton donated $1 million to help develop a coronavirus vaccine." *New York Times*, November 18, 2020.

*Guerrero, Gene. "Dolly Parton and Porter Wagoner: . . . It's Awfully Hard to Just Let Them People Go By In The World And Not Say Something About It." *The Great Speckled Bird*, May 17, 1971.

*Hurst, Jack. "Dolly Parton: Pushing forward through the fear." *Chicago Tribune*, January 31, 1976, 11.

*Watts, Cindy. "Dolly Parton pledges additional $3 million to Tennessee fire victims." *USA Today*, May 5, 2017.

Acknowledgments

A heap of thanks to:

DJ for the dazzlin' book idea;

Carolyn Yoder for bringing it to life;

Lydia Hamessley, professor of music at Hamilton College and author of *Unlikely Angel: The Songs of Dolly Parton*;

David Dotson at The Dollywood Foundation for his assistance on the project;

and the tireless, generous, fabulous Dolly, whose incredible talent still shines brighter than a thousand fireflies on a moonless night.